To: Rev. Leonard Jackson

May God richly bless you
as you continue to bless others

Thank you and Many
Blessings

Melissa McClain

I battled the fear that once lived within me and for a season it did retreat; but when it came back with a vengeance to conquer, I declared...

"Simpleton, I will _never_ be beat!"

\- Melissa McCloud

Determined to **Live**....
Without
Fear

**How to Boldly, Confidently, & Fearlessly
Live your Life!**

Melissa McCloud

Determined to Live Without Fear

This book is available at quantity discounts for regular/bulk purchase.

For more information contact:
Up Close Publishing
PO Box 881344, Los Angeles, CA 90009

Website: MelissaMcCloud.com

Book Melissa McCloud today to perform & speak to your group, organization, school, or event from her motivational series;
"Be Bold, Be Confident, and Be Fearlessly You!"

For Bookings send an email to:
Booking@MelissaMcCloud.com

Melissa McCloud also online at:
Myspace.com/MelissaMcCloud

Melissa McCloud's Music Downloads & Products available on:
ITunes, Napster, Rhapsody, eMusic, and Amazon

Online ordering is available for all products.
Published By: Up Close Publishing
Copyright ©2009 by: Melissa McCloud

All Rights Reserved
First Edition
Printed in the United States of America

Scripture quotations are taken from: King James Version (KJV), New King James Version (NKJV), and the New International Version (NIV) of the Bible.

Library of Congress Cataloging-in-Publication Data
McCloud, Melissa
Determined to Live Without Fear:
How to Boldly, Confidently, and Fearlessly Live Your Life

ISBN 13: 978-0-615-30936-1
ISBN 10: 0-615-309336-4
Library of Congress Control Number: 2009932525

Dedicated to the Reader:

May this book help guide you on your journey to living fearlessly!

Acknowledgements

First and foremost I acknowledge and thank my Heavenly Father whose love and guidance has given me the hope, understanding, joy, peace, and courage to live my divine destiny. It is in Him that I have discovered who I really am and learned how to love, forgive, and have faith. I know that with Him nothing is impossible, His love is limitless, and that He is always with me!

I would like to thank my father, Eddie McCloud, for being the best father that I could have asked for. Dad, you have been the strong mountain, the quiet wind beneath my wings, the solid foundation to our family's livelihood and; whose love, support, and faith in God has helped me to be the best that I can be! Because you are in my life, I know how to love and I know what it means to sacrifice for your family. Because of you, I know how to live a balanced life, how stand up for what I believe in, how to be a good parent when I become one, and most importantly you have encouraged me to follow what is in my heart. I love you daddy, and I truly hope that you know how wonderful you have been to me, our family, and a true blessing to many from God.

I'd like to thank my loving mother, Dr. Zyra McCloud, for praying for my "arrival" and for praying for me daily as I walk faithfully throughout my journey of life. I am an extension of you and we share a kindred spirit of love and peace for all of mankind. Mom, you are the greatest mother that I could have ever asked God for and it is because of your unwavering love, guidance, support, fellowship, prayers, actions, and faith that have encouraged me to wholeheartedly strive to be the best that I can be. You have been a light in my life and in the lives of so many others. I appreciate and love you, and thank God Almighty for creating you. Your life is truly a blessing to the world!

I'd like to thank my loving newlywed sister, Tamekia White, for your unconditional love and support. You are one of the most selfless people that I know. You are truly a divine gift to the world, a faithful servant, and a woman of God. You give and encourage from your heart and I know that everyone who has an opportunity to meet you or who is in your presence is truly blessed. I'd also like to thank my brother-in-law Gartrell White for supporting me and my music, for your sincerity and loving heart, and for being a wonderful new family member, friend, and husband to my sister.

I'd like to thank my Godmother, Annie Thomas, for her steadfast love and support of me since I was a baby. I thank you for hanging up my posters on your wall and for displaying my Music CD's & pictures on your TV stand. Believe it or not it's sometimes the little things that you do and say that touch the very heart of me. I'd also like to thank you for being an extended mother to me and others for it is because of you that we all are loved in an extra special way.

I'd like to thank my beloved friend, Joseph Trower, whose friendship, management, and encouragement has been unwavering and truly marvelous in my life. You have been consistent in speaking of your faith in our Heavenly Father. Your unfailing encouraging words and belief in me to sing, perform, and to write this book have been a great inspiration to me and I thank you for being a loving person and exceptional friend.

I'd also like to thank some of my dearest friends: Jaiden Taylor (my spiritual sister) your prayers and support have changed my life; Sherita Marks-Pearson, (one of my best friends) for your love and for being a friend to me since we were in fifth grade and to her children; my godkids Tamon Pearson, Shardonnay Pearson, and also to their eldest brother Trejon Pearson; to my divinely cherished friend, Joe Marcelino, (an awesome man of God) for your encouraging words and faith in me to minister through music. It has been a pleasure performing with you and reaching out to people with positive messages in Music & Video; to my godsister Pamela Briggs, for your support and encouraging words and faith in me to achieve my dreams; to my godsister Jeanine Taylor and parents Tina and John Taylor, for being close friends of the family and for all of your love and support; to Lynette Hill, you have always believed in me and saw a greater vision of me sometimes greater than I saw of myself; to my uncle Johnnie Nelson; to Carolyn McNeil and her Husband James Taylor and my goddaughter Arianna Taylor; and to Neil McNeil and Momma McNeil, for all of your consistent encouraging words and prayers. Thank you, for you all have truly made a difference in my life.

And to Mark Anthony Smith; Reverend Murrelle Garr; Davita Roberts; Thai Long Ly; Nate Pleasure; Uncle Alton McCloud and family; My brother Eddie McCloud and his wife Susan McCloud and their children; my nieces and nephews Jessica McCloud, Matthew McCloud, Mariah McCloud, Eddie McCloud Jr.; Ann Earl; Cleda McKenzie; Stephanie Rolle; Tracy Lipscomb; Vinnie Ratcliff; PA Edmead; Louis Abrigo; Revlyn Williams; Sharon & Esther Odiakosa; John and Rita Polk; and to all of my family, friends, and associates—I'd like to thank you all for your kind words and/or support that you have given me over the years.

And last but not least, I want to thank all of you who have purchased and/or reading this book. Because of your support, your life has made a difference in my life and I believe that your very existence is an extension of God's love. I appreciate you and thank you for your support and wish you all the very best that life can offer!

Always From my Heart to Yours,
Melissa McCloud

Contents

Contents

PREFACE

Every day is a journey for me as I am determined to live my life without fear, doubt, worry, and frustration. This book was birthed out of my own personal challenges, my desire to encourage others to overcome their perceived limitations, and by the direction of my "spiritual higher self," to overcome low self-esteem, fear, and negative thinking.

I know that there is hope in every situation and we can find inspiration in various ways, such as by reading books, through prayer and meditation, exercising faith, through our own personal spoken and written affirmations, and from encouragement from our family and friends.

However, as often as we can be encouraged, at times we can also find ourselves being discouraged. Generally, discouragement affects us when forget to re-affirm the fact that nothing stays the same, and that ultimately we have the power within us to improve our lives and change our circumstances.

There is power in what we think. There is power in what we say. There is power in what we do and there is power when we allow ourselves to release the power that has already been abundantly supplied within us.

So, by knowing this, when I am faced with challenges that would try to discourage me, I remind myself daily of the God-given talents and truths that are found within me. I know that I must not meditate on thoughts of worry, doubts, fears, and disbeliefs.

Living life without pre-imposed fears, empowers you to live with boldness, confidence, and with assurance that you can freely live the "abundant life" of your choosing!

Living a bold, confident, and fearless life is a daily walk. So I would encourage you, as I have, to read this book daily and read through it as many times as you can. I believe that the words of encouragement found within its pages can become a foundational fortitude of power that re-confirms the authority, ability, privileges, and power that you already have within you.

INTRODUCTION

It had taken years for me to finally see that the life that I live is the life that I have chosen to live. I choose everyday when I wake up if I am going to feel happy, grateful, pessimistic, optimistic, fearful, or bold. I had once believed that I had no power over my circumstances, i.e., my finances, my career, my relationships, etc., but one morning I woke up and realized that I do have the power. I realized that everything that I needed for my aspirations to come to pass was already on the inside of me. I just had to access it!

For so long I held on to this way of feeling mediocre. I operated and somewhat believed that it was okay just to get by on what little I had. I was always hoping for the best but not really believing I deserved or could have it. In my youth, I was criticized and ostracized by my peers for being what they perceived as different from them and thus I feared allowing myself to really be the best that I could be. I knew if I walked upright with my shoulders squared back and my chin up that people would take more notice of me. And I knew if I spoke boldly and unafraid on how I felt about certain issues, that I may be subjected to possible debates. I didn't want that. I wanted people to like me. I wanted to be accepted, respected, and recognized for who I was. The only problem was I didn't accept myself.

What I've observed over time is that people admire and respect people who are confident, bold, and true to who they are. Anyone can be passive, but it takes courage and confidence to be bold and fearless! People see you as you see yourself, and however you think about yourself is what you will exude. This was not an easy task, and not something accomplished overnight. I had to work on changing the way I thought about myself.

One way I did this was by looking in the mirror everyday and taking notice of all of my beautiful features. I began to practice walking tall and putting on the nice dresses and shoes that would accentuate my figure and make me feel fabulous. I started working more and more on my talents and meditating and thinking on ways that I could approach my career differently. I began to think of all of my unique qualities and what I already had inside of me that could be a major blessing to people.

One thing I knew for sure was that I had to become a walking "billboard" for the attributes I would represent and to embrace releasing the true me to the world indefinitely. I had to learn to accept who I am, appreciate all of my characteristics, love myself unconditionally, and be the best that I could be! I had to discover and fully accept that it was ok for me to be bold, confident, and fearlessly me.

I know that this is my life and I am excited about it! Every day is a new day and I am excited about all of the possibilities that life has to offer. I decided that I was no longer going to be afraid to be the best that I could be. I was no longer going to be afraid to speak with confidence and shy away from who I really am. I was no longer going to be afraid to be confidently me wherever I go. As a matter of fact, I wanted to be noticed because if I am noticed perhaps people will be inspired to be bold and confident as well.

When people see me not only do I want them to see a bold, confident, and fearless woman, but I want them to see someone who has love in her heart. That is why I am writing this book so that people will know that it's okay to be the best that they can be, to love themselves, to love God, and to love one another. There are people in this world and possibly around you that need love, motivating, and encouraging. It doesn't matter if they are rich or poor, tall or short, thin or curvy, religious or not—we all need love.

So, I want to encourage you to let your imprint in life be one of love, courage, and freedom. Be liberated to let your light shine in the world and know without a shadow of doubt that it is absolutely, positively, okay for you to be Bold, Confident, and Fearlessly all that you can be!

I.

CONQUER YOUR FEARS

"The illusion of fear negates the unleashed truths within...release them and ignite your passion (s)."

- Melissa McCloud

Principle # 1

Believe in

Yourself

Believe in Yourself

Everything that you need to be successful and to follow your dreams is already on the inside of you. But first, you have to believe in yourself.

There is a wealth of abundance within you that is waiting to be discovered and ignited! When you believe in yourself, you will find the power within you to boldly conquer your fears and doubts, to think beyond your perceived limitations, and to use your mind, thoughts, and actions to ignite your purpose, faith, goals, and objectives.

There is nothing too great or too small that can't be done! Whatever you want to create, design, build, perform, or achieve, you can. The world is filled with limitless possibilities and there are many people who know this and who are living it! Think of all the wonderful inventions, gadgets, computers, cars, electronic devices, and much more that are being produced and sold worldwide every day. Technology is rapidly growing and today's society is full of information that is made available to us through the Internet, books, libraries, and videos.

Every one of us has power within us to create change in our lives. Here are some points that will help you to ignite your power within:

#1 – **Believe in yourself -** If you don't believe in yourself, it makes it difficult for others to believe differently.

Believe in Yourself

#2 – Speak positive things about yourself - Words are very powerful and can create great change in your life.

#3 – Be bold - Actively pursue your dreams, goals, and ambitions without doubt, and know that you can achieve them!

#4 – Manage your thoughts - Focus and meditate daily on your personal strengths, characteristics, and qualities that you can utilize to bring you closer to your goals.

#5 – Engage your passion(s) - Engage in activities that promote your passions, build on your dreams, and enhance your strengths. Fulfillment in different areas of your life often come when you engage in activities that promote what you are passionate about and that of which makes you happy within.

There is no dream too big or too small! It doesn't matter your background, color, religion or creed. You can obtain whatever you set your mind to do. If you want to build the tallest building on the planet you can. If you want to build the fastest airplane you can, and as peculiar as this may seem if you wanted to build a car that can fly… you can.

Create and shape your own destiny. Define your life by embracing the power within you by loving yourself, thinking positive thoughts, and knowing without a shadow of doubt that nothing is impossible to them that believe and work towards it.

Principle # 1
Believe in Yourself

Remember, you are one of a kind with talents that the world is waiting for. Make the best of your life by utilizing your talents and skills to go forth and show the world what you are made of! Be encouraged, you have the power within you to live freely in a world with endless possibilities! Whatever you set your mind to do you can achieve it! Think positive thoughts, speak your personal affirmations daily, and know without a shadow of doubt that you deserve the very best that life has to offer!

> ***Affirmation*** *- something that is affirmed; a statement or proposition that is declared to be true; to express agreement with or commitment to; uphold; support.*

Turn your thoughts into action and your actions into accomplishing what you believe. This is your life, your season, and your time to be the very best that you can be! The time is now; don't wait until tomorrow to start believing in yourself. Within you are mounds of talents, skills, and desires that are waiting for you to activate them with your thoughts, actions, and commitment. The champion is already within you and with commitment and consistency in achieving your goals you'll find that the guarantees of dedication and sacrifice were well worth the benefits and rewards!

> *"Believe in yourself... you can change your life!"*
> *-Melissa McCloud*

Principle # 2

Discover the Purpose of Your Life

Principle # 2
Discover the Purpose of Your Life

Believe it or not, you were born and created to live your own unique purpose in life. The timing of your birth was pre-calculated and divinely orchestrated by God from the time you were born here on earth until the time you will depart earth.

Your life is not an accident, happenstance, or mere coincidence. You were divinely created and purposed by God to live your life with the fullness of faith and confidence in His power, and meant to embrace your life as one of purpose and significance.

> *"Before I formed you in the womb I knew you, before you were born I set you apart; I appointed you as a prophet to the nations." Jeremiah 1:5 (NIV)*

First let me explain, that the word "purpose" used in this text is not used in a singular tense. I do not believe that you were created to only complete "a singular" purpose in life. "The Purpose of Your Life" is used to describe the many attributes, successes, contributions, and rewards that you will offer and receive throughout the course of your life happenings. There are many people you will encounter whose lives you will affect and the accumulation of your life's experiences will embody what is known as "the purpose of your life."

So how do you find out what your purpose in life is? Everything that has ever been invented, created, or designed was developed with a purpose in mind by the one who created it. The creator designed it to have certain functions, qualities, capabilities, and physical appearances to serve that

31

in which it was created to do. In essence, you were created to serve a purpose, or perhaps many purposes, in life. Your structural body design, talents, skills, characteristics, personality traits, passions, and desires were all created and developed within you to serve a purpose.

However, to fully seek and discover your purpose you will have to find the answer from the one who created you. In fact, we are all God's creations and to discover God's purpose for your life you must seek His direction and wisdom in all things. A contented life that is driven by divine purpose is found by seeking His guidance and by allowing your inner spiritual self to reveal your purpose filled daily instructions.

Finding your purpose may take some time and often is commonly found by living through life's experiences. However, along the way you must trust that no matter what occurrences you experience, they are a part of your life's journey and that in every situation or experience you can choose to progress or digress your efforts.

Many of the things that we experience in life are based on our choices to act in accordance with our higher-self or to choose to act based in our fears and doubts. The setbacks or successes that are yielded in our lives undoubtedly occur from the formations of our daily decisions.

If you understand or know your purpose in life you must realize that everything that you've experienced has happened for a purpose. For example, being laid off from your job could be an opportunity for promotion at another job or to start your

Discover the Purpose of Your Life

own business. Or, perhaps you ended a relationship with someone to potentially meet another person whose presence in your life will be more rewarding! Seeking and discovering your purpose in life will yield a lifetime of continuous discoveries.

> *"But seek ye first the kingdom of God, and his righteousness; and all these things shall be added unto you."*
> *Matthew 6:33 (KJV)*

Begin to seek divine direction, wisdom, and understanding in all things from the Creator and watch the purposes of your life begin to unfold and become apparent and clear. Once you allow His guidance to direct your path, you will experience a heightened level of peace, love, understanding, and comfort by knowing that your true purpose in life is in the purpose of Him that created you and to allow everything that you need to be found within Him.

The purpose of your life is in your everyday walk through life's explorations. As previously mentioned, everything that you need is already found within you and as you have been purposed to read the pages of this book, I believe that you are destined to accomplish, overcome, and create more than you could imagine or think!

Your life was created with great significance and power. You must trust your instincts, align with your higher spiritually-guided self and know that you were intently created and formed to live a life filled with purpose, and that purpose is found in God.

Principle # 3

Release Your Fears

Release Your Fears

Would you love yourself enough to continue to move forward with your goals and dreams against all odds, fears, and naysayers? One of the most difficult challenges I had in the past was knowing in my heart what I was supposed to do with my career but not being able to complete my projects due to initially not having the necessary financial income. My debt was growing and I was becoming increasingly afraid to pursue what was in my heart. I knew I was supposed to trust God—as I regularly asked Him to show me the way—but it still took a while before I knew exactly what to do and what direction to take.

What do you do when fear tells you to quit? Sometimes, you may want to give up because you can't see how something is going to change or happen. Sure, you go to church and hear a good message, or you've listened to motivational tapes and read inspiring books; but what happens when you have to face your same problems again and again, day after day, and your difficulties seem unwavering? You may feel alone, somewhat abandoned, and slightly depressed, worrying about how you are going to make it through each day. Maybe you want to give in to your fears, throw in the towel and say "forget it," but something inside you just won't let you lose hope.

Fear- *a distressing emotion; that which causes a feeling of being afraid; concern or anxiety; solicitude.*

In the Holy Bible it reads, *"God has not given us the spirit of fear but of power and of love, and of sound mind," (2 Timothy 1:7, NKJV).*

Release Your Fears

I believe that He is right there with you, hoping that you will resist the fear and the temptation to quit. It is important to not increase your fears with doubt and disbelief because you are more than likely closer to the breakthrough that you have been praying for and working towards. Just imagine Angels in Heaven cheering for you to continue to never lose hope and singing songs of victory just for you!

There are many challenges that we face in life that may cultivate fear. However, the only way you can allow "fear" to win is if you allow your life decisions to be made based on what you fear. Let me repeat that... The only way you can allow "fear" to win is if you allow your life decisions to be made based on what you fear. You can take action against your fears right now by not letting them influence you from having the faith and courage to move ahead. Every time you make decisions contrary to what you fear you empower yourself and weaken your fears.

F.E.A.R - "False- Evidence -Appearing -Real"

I am growing and learning every day, and I am striving to be the best that I can to fulfill my life's ultimate purpose. I have learned that my primary hindrance to living an abundant life was by allowing my fears to dominate my thoughts, decisions, and belief in myself.

Some people have fears that prevent them from ending an unhealthy relationship, leaving a job that they detest, quitting a bad habit, eradicating negative thinking, loving themselves, or positioning themselves to be as successful as they can be. Yes, that's correct, some people are afraid to allow

Release Your Fears

themselves to do what it takes to be successful in their careers, relationships, and goals. However, I want you to be encouraged to never let fear stop you from doing what is in your heart and living your life's purpose. You are a winner and you have the power within you to succeed at whatever you set your mind to do. The more you take action against your fears the more they will disappear.

Everyone can make various decisions to empower themselves by releasing their fears to live with confidence. Always remember that inside of you is courage, strength, originality, hope, and power; so it is now time to allow yourself to be fearless and to enjoy all of the love, peace, joy, success, wealth, and good health that living a "fearless" life can bring.

If you have an idea, vision, or a task that must be completed—go for it! Keep moving forward and don't look back. Don't worry about how it is all going to come together. If you are divinely ordered to complete an assignment and you stay in faith to complete it—even against unseemly odds—you will succeed!

A scripture in the bible found in Joshua 1:9, KJV reads, *"Be strong and of good Courage, be neither afraid nor dismayed: for the Lord your God is with you wherever you go".* The scripture is true and if a thought comes into your mind that causes you to fear say this affirmation boldly and aloud every day; **"I am not afraid for God has not given me the spirit of fear. I am a victor and not a victim. I am bold, I am confident, and I am fearlessly me!"**

Principle # 3

Release Your Fears

Release your fears, embrace your power, and determine today in your mind and in your heart that you are going to complete your goals, dreams, and objectives until the very end. Faith is what pleases God and unwavering faith is what brings about an expedient change. Faith is the opponent to fear! The most effective way to combat fear is to have rooted faith within yourself that you will not give fear any permission or power to operate in your life.

Write down your goals and prepare yourself daily to accomplish them. Remember, don't give up, don't give in, and don't you dare quit, because you just may be getting closer to the promotion and reward that living a fearless life can bring!

II.

IGNITE YOUR CONFIDENCE

"The time is now! Seize the day.

Embrace your life and live it your way.

Remember it starts with you!"

- Melissa McCloud

Principle # 4

Don't Quit

Don't Quit

Have you ever begun a project, an assignment, a goal, or something you started but didn't finish it and when looking back in retrospect wished you could have gone back to complete it? Or perhaps you ran a race or participated in a competition that you didn't win and later found yourself giving up on the hope or possibility of ever winning.

If this describes some of your experiences and you have wanted to give up on your hopes and your dreams, then I want you to know, that within you, is the power and ability to be a success at whatever level you set your mind to be. Now, I know it's easy sometimes to throw in the towel, wave the white flag, and walk away from your goals when things get tough, but don't you dare quit! Let me repeat that... DON'T QUIT!

There were times when I wanted to give up on my goals and career plans. Nothing seemed to be going the way I'd hoped and planned. I wasn't selling my music CD's from my first album in the volumes that I had hoped and my monies were depleted. I wasn't really motivated to do anything differently than what I had started which at that time was performing at shows and singing my original songs. My love life had uncertainties. My car was scheduled to be repossed. I couldn't pay rent for my apartment. Creditors were calling consistently about loans that needed to be repaid and I'd wonder with all of this, how I could possibly be on the right track. I was ready to quit on pursuing my career goals and give into my fears. However something inside of me just wouldn't let me quit. Every time I thought of quitting, I would remind myself that my life was ultimately not about me.

Don't Quit

My gifts and talents were not just for me to keep to myself but were to be used to inspire other people as well. Reminding myself daily of this truth would help to renew my faith that I could achieve anything that I set my mind to do.

I believe in the power of prayer, so I would ask God what path I should take and what talents should I use to fulfill my divinely guided purpose. Once my path became clear I knew I couldn't quit. With His guidance I knew that I couldn't go wrong and no matter what my circumstances looked like, everything would be alright.

If you continue to work towards your goals and ambitions, you'll find a great comfort when you can let go of your fears and trust that all things will eventually align themselves for your benefit. Prayer and my trust in God's help certainly comforted me; however, I would also encourage you that even if you don't pray, to listen to that positive inner voice sometimes described as your "conscious" and use it to keep you motivated.

Never give up on your hopes, dreams, or ambitions even when the challenges you encounter seem too difficult to conquer. Never give up because you just may be on the edge of a breakthrough or at the point where your challenges will take a turn for the better.

At a point in my life I had to embark on a journey whereas I didn't have a definite idea of what will happen along the way and honestly at times I felt afraid. But, I decided to ignore my fears and make choices that would eventually offer great recompense.

Don't Quit

Truly, it is common at first to fear the "unknown" along with the uncertainties that we face in our lives, but what separates us from the conquerors and the defeated is if we allow what we fear to solely determine our decisions.

I want to encourage you to let nothing or no one influence you to make a decision contrary to what is in your heart and contrary to your life's purpose and objectives. You have to live with it-- not them. The truth is there are no unknowns—just different outcomes that will arise based on the decisions we make. Or rather, you have many paths to choose from and at the end of each path you will find a different result. We always have a choice to empower ourselves by boldly and fearlessly making choices that will produce our desired results.

No matter how difficult your challenges, always remember that nothing stays the same. Just as the seasons change so do our lives. I have learned not to worry about things that I cannot change and to focus more on changing the things that I can. Every day is a new day so exercise your power daily to confidently and fearlessly choose to act in accordance with your goals, convictions, and beliefs.

Don't quit! Become a finisher and finish your project, tasks, and goals. Greatness is not so much measured by the one who finishes the quickest but to the one who endures to the end. Set your goals, see them through, and never quit working towards being bold, confident, and fearlessly you!

Principle # 5

Dare to be

Fabulous

Dare to be Fabulous

Do you believe that you deserve to live your life feeling beautiful, confident, happy, secure in your own skin, successful in your career, and loved with people around you to share it with? Hopefully your answer is yes, because you deserve to look and feel fabulous!

Feeling fabulous is not so much what appears on the outside but rather how you feel about yourself on the inside and what you believe you are deserving of. Living a "fabulous life," begins with believing that you, like anyone else, can live your life looking and feeling your best; with love, confidence, boldness, determination, fearlessness, and resolve.

When challenges and obstacles arise, see them as opportunities to learn from and know that you have the power to overcome them. We are all growing and learning daily and it is not so much what happens to us when facing challenges but how we react to those challenges. Every day you have the power to make decisions that will either take you one step forward or two steps backwards. You have the privilege to choose to live a fabulous life, so let's start today!

No matter your shape, size, skin color, facial features, ethnicity, or age, you can look and feel fabulous every day. Remember, feeling fabulous and looking good is more of an attitude than an appearance so if you feel beautiful and confident on the inside, it will resonate on the outside. People will notice your comeliness, acknowledge your confidence, and more than likely compliment you for your efforts.

Dare to be Fabulous

So how do begin to feel confident on the inside? First, you must know that what you see in the mirror everyday is simply a reflection of the thoughts you hold in your mind. You must believe within you that you are perfectly made just the way you are. Say this affirmation daily, **"I am beautifully and wonderfully made."**   Every time you look in the mirror, take a little time to appreciate your individual physical features and think about all the wonderful internal qualities that you have within.

> ***Fabulous*** *– incredible; astounding; exceptionally good; marvelous; superb.*

Every day practice standing up straight with your shoulders squared back and your chin up. This will help to boost your self-confidence and your outward appearance. The more you practice this the more natural it will feel to you. Walking with proper posture also strengthens your shoulders and back and it accentuates your confidence as well. Remember to always walk with confidence. When you walk with confidence it shows people that you feel good about yourself and is a surefire way to stand out!

Also, when you look good you feel good, so strive to look and feel your best daily. Put on your best outfits (and don't keep them in the closet forever waiting for a special occasion that rarely comes), add a little make up to enhance your beauty, splash on a little cologne, put on the shoes that make you feel fabulous, and go out and strut your stuff!

Dare to be Fabulous

Take time daily to speak positive things about yourself. This is important because the more you speak your encouraging affirmations the more you will begin to internalize them and eventually your actions will align with them. Be the best that you can be. Believe in yourself and live your life knowing that you have everything within you to be bold, confident, and fearlessly free!

Let the world see the fabulous you. You were born for an extraordinary purpose and you have the power to create and choose the life that you desire to live. Set your mind and thoughts to believe that you deserve and are capable of living "a fabulous life."

Say this affirmation daily;

"There is no other like me. I am beautiful, bold, and confidently me. Today I choose to be the best that I can be and exude my fabulousness for all to see!"

Truthfully, you are…one of a kind on both the inside and out. You are unique in your own special way and once you align yourself in accordance with the totality of your uniqueness; your confidence and beliefs will undoubtedly begin to unveil the powerful, fearless, and fabulous side of you.

You must never hold back from being the best individual that you can be. Always embrace the essence of your inner and outer fabulousness and let everyone who is in your presence see the bold, confident, and fearlessly fabulous person that you have allowed yourself to be!

Principle # 6

Listen to Your Body

Listen to Your Body

For much of my life I'd struggled with the fluctuation of my weight. Since I was twelve years old I would constantly get on the scale hoping that I didn't gain a few pounds here and there. I'd ask a few friends every so often, "Do I look fat in this?" after putting on clothes. I exercised often but would never really reach my ideal weight goal. The reality is that I knew what foods would promote weight gain and those foods that would keep me healthy, but I had very little discipline in the area of listening to my body when determining what foods I would intently indulge. It can be stressful worrying about weight gain and weight loss every day. Therefore it is more advantageous to focus on loving yourself enough to make decisions initially that will offer your body and health a great reward.

When I stopped focusing on trying to lose weight and just made it a lifestyle to eat properly and exercise, my body automatically started shaping up and my excess weight began to disappear. Hooray! The secret is to listen to your body. Make a choice daily to drink plenty of water, eat healthy, and of course partake in some form of exercise.

You can engage in exercise by walking, swimming, dancing (my favorite), bowling, skiing, roller skating, basketball, cheerleading, soccer, or whatever you like to do that will get you off of the couch and moving. Eating healthy foods combined with exercising will help you to look good and feel great!

Be consistent and persistent when working to achieve your fitness goals. Every day that you exercise and eat healthy

Listen to Your Body

you are just that much closer to your goal. Keep a journal of your physical activities and of the foods that you eat daily. Journaling your food intake will help you to stay on track by observing what foods you should keep in and out of your diet. Also, take notice of the foods that make you feel great and those that cause slothfulness. When you are tempted to indulge in something that would ignite weight gain or weight loss, depending on your personal goals, think twice and ask yourself if it is worthy of what you will gain in return. Decide whether the food would add or subtract from the time and efforts that you have exerted daily toward your goal. Ask yourself, "Is this food worthy of me?"

The key to reaching your desired physical goal is to resolve in your mind, body, and soul with determination and conviction that you will undoubtedly live the life you are intended to live that is free of bondage to foods and habits that repeatedly bring you to a constant state of physical stagnation and emotional regret. For every action there is a reaction, so you must decide whether or not the reaction that will be produced as a result of your action is worth the possible long term effect that your action will bring.

You should not live your life constantly worrying if you are too fat or too skinny, but instead live at your highest potential and highest level of self-esteem. It is imperative to decrease focusing on weight loss or weight gain and focus more intently on finding the peace and awareness of your essential existence. Determine the foods, exercises, and activities that make you feel healthy and physically empowered and make your choices accordingly.

Listen to Your Body

Remember that a short moment of indulgence can cause a longer time of restoration. Whatever your temptation or habit is, you have the power to choose to engage in it or resist it. The good news is the more you resist the temptation to indulge in an unsatisfactory habit or "guilty pleasure," the more you weaken your desire for it!

Take notice of your body's likes and dislikes and adhere to them because they are key links to your physical and mental success. Make the decision that you will be a champion for your health and an advocate for continually looking and feeling your best.

Every day you have a choice of what you will eat and drink, what physical activities you will partake in, and what you will allow to dominate your sub-conscious thoughts. Take charge of your health and decide today that change and commitment begins with you. You have the power to listen to your body and prove to yourself that you have the determination, courage, and tenacity to see your goals through. It may take a little time or maybe no time at all but if you want to see change, remember it starts with you!

III.

PREPARE FOR SUCCESS

"It is the little steps daily that brings about the greatest changes infinitely!"

- Melissa McCloud

Principle # 7

Use Your Talents

Principle #7

Use Your Talents

You are unique, gifted, and talented in your own way. There are characteristics and individual qualities that you posses that distinguishes you from everyone else.

What is it that you love to do? What are you skilled in doing? What comes naturally to you or is easy for you to do? This may be a good indication of your talents! Once you discover and acknowledge your talents, cultivate them. Strive to be the best at them. Focus on developing your talent and skills and try not to compare your talent to someone else's.

Your talents are all your own and the world is waiting for you to embrace, develop, and share them. Make the necessary time in your daily schedule to contribute to your talents and goals. If you have to practice, study, train, rehearse, memorize, exercise, or any other activity that you need to set aside time for, then set your mind that you are going to go for it and give it all you got!

Now I've heard some people say, "I don't have any talents," and "I don't know what I want to do with my life." Then I would respond, "What are some of the things that you don't like and would like to see changed in the world?" Perhaps an issue or something that you'd like to see changed in the world could be a clue as to what you may be gifted in and purposed to change.

Know that you are a valuable person with much to offer within the world around you. Your life is significant and you were born for a divine purpose. Feel confident about the talent and skills that you possess and be proud just to be you!

Use Your Talents

By confidently and boldly making use of your talents and skills you not only will you be an inspiration to yourself but to people all around you. Believe it or not, there are people who are waiting for you to boldly, confidently, and fearlessly go forth and release your inner power. They are waiting to be blessed by all of your talents, skills and gifts. Be proud of the innate talent and skills that you have within and don't be afraid to share them with those around you. Work daily to strengthen your talents and skills and when the opportunity comes for you to share them, take full advantage of the opportunity.

Because we all have individual qualities, you must never feel or believe that anyone is greater than you. You must never feel inferior to anyone because we all live and breathe, and are integral parts of humankind. You must know that you deserve to be treated at all times with dignity and respect, and you must always present yourself accordingly in the same manner. Surely, there are many people who are known for their vast achievements and have gained much notoriety but it is important for you to know that when you are living your life's purpose you are who you were created to be. You are not a carbon copy of someone else. Your gifts and your talents are all your own, and you were distinctly created to use the talent and skills that are already bound within you!

There is an interesting story in the Holy Bible that describes three servants who were given talents (referring to money) by their master (boss) according to their abilities. Out of the three servants, one of the servants took his talent and hid it, whereby not cultivating it or increasing it. The other two servants who received talents according to their abilities

Use Your Talents

multiplied them instead of hiding them, and made their master proud. However their master was disappointed with the servant who buried and hid his talent instead of increasing it and as a result of his lack of productivity he was banished (fired) and forced to never return again. *(Parable found in Matthew 25: 14-39, KJV)*

So in essence, you must prepare yourself to use your God-given talents and embrace the world with all the privileges and promotions that lay within. Your talents are gifts to you from our Creator to share with those around you—so don't hide them. Engage them for the benefit of others and in turn your talents will promote you.

Set your mind daily on accomplishing or working towards all things necessary to bring you closer to your goals. Keep in mind that it is up to you to use your talents and release your ambitions to rise up and project your higher self and highest potential.

Principle # 8

Get Ready for

Opportunity

Principle # 8
Get Ready for Opportunity

If you were to encounter an unexpected yet hoped-for opportunity that could change your life, would you be prepared to take advantage of it? Would you have taken the necessary time to prepare yourself to be successful in your career, goals, and aspirations? Many times opportunities can arise when you least expect it. The old adage, "Success comes when opportunity meets preparation," is very true, and so it is important for you to always be prepared. Don't delay performing and executing the necessary work that must be done in order for you to achieve your goals and to prepare you for an opportunity that will help further your objectives.

Have you ever heard someone say, "Shoot, if only I knew that would happen, I would have been prepared," or "How could I have not been prepared for that opportunity?" You must motivate and encourage yourself daily to plan and prepare ahead for an expected or unexpected opportunity. Therefore, if you are challenged with procrastination, set a timeline and focus your attention on completing one goal at a time. Many times, there are so many things that we'd like to accomplish that we often try accomplishing them all at the same time. However, the downside to focusing on achieving multiple goals simultaneously is that it can often lead to inadequate attention and low performance towards completing each individual goal.

Advanced preparation is vital to being prepared when an opportunity presents itself. Every day take some time to do whatever is necessary that will bring you closer to your dreams and goals.   If it is exercising, reading, studying, rehearsing, training, practicing, writing or whatever is

71

required—do it. Don't hesitate, don't procrastinate, and don't deter from utilizing your time wisely.

Keep a daily journal or calendar where you can write down what you've accomplished each day. This will help you keep note of your progress. How you manage your time is a key factor to your success, so write down your goals on paper and as you complete each goal check off that it was done. If you set a goal for the day and were unable to finish it, that is okay. Put it on your daily plan for the following day and try your best to accomplish it at that time. If you do manage to fulfill all the goals for a specific day, be proud of yourself that you stuck to your plan and that you took another step on the pathway to success.

In addition, be mindful and cautious of people and things that will cause distractions or that will take you off of your daily plan. Try your best to avoid them. If needed, plan leisure time in your day where distractions may be allowed.

Make a commitment to yourself that daily you are going to work towards preparing yourself for the plans that you would like to see accomplished and for the success that you will become. Begin to envision yourself successful and equipped so that when an opportunity comes you are pre-prepared for victory!

Keep yourself grounded and surrounded with positive people and things. Networking and connecting with people in your field of work will help you to successfully establish a network base of contacts.

Get Ready for Opportunity

It's also good to find a mentor in your career field who is established and renowned in their line of work so that you can learn from their experiences. Ideally, by studying and observing what other people have done successfully to reach their goals in your career field can also help you to learn varying ideas and insight to approaches that may have not yet been utilized.

Every day take some time to think and meditate on your affirmations. Think about your goals and how you'd like to achieve them. Read books that will motivate you and expand your mind to limitless possibilities. As for me, I love to read books that are inspirational and that encourage me to live an abundant life. My favorite is the Holy Bible. Every day I try to read a chapter or a scripture than offers me insight, encouragement, and hope towards my life's daily experiences.

When surrounding myself with people on a daily basis, I choose to cultivate relationships with those people who share similar ideals as me, who are positive, supportive, and who respect me as a person. Even when I turn on the TV, I really like to watch television shows and movies that are inspirational. I love watching stories of famous people's lives and how they achieved success. Their stories really encourage me because I've learned that many of them have had some of the same challenges that I've faced, and that they overcame their obstacles with hard work, confidence, boldness, and dedication. Frankly, nothing really makes them different from you or me. Every one of us has the capacity to rise above our current circumstances if we stay persistent and consistent in seeing our goals through.

Get Ready for Opportunity

Always remember that the time that you have to utilize daily towards working towards your goals, is one of the most valuable resources that you have.   Therefore, it is necessary that you maximize your time so that it is used productively because; what you do today determines the outcomes of your tomorrow and how you make daily use of your time is vital to your success!

Principle # 9

Evaluate the Company You Keep

Evaluate the Company You Keep

Many times we hold in our sub-conscious mind and thoughts information that we have seen and/or heard without consciously realizing that we have internalized it. In essence, everything that you see and hear will have an effect on you in some way. Additionally, those individuals who are around you every day, whether it be your friends, family members, co-workers, or acquaintances-- each of them will possess some level of influence in your life whether you are cognizant of it or not.

This is why it is important to closely associate and align yourself with people who can be of a positive influence. Understandably, you may have to work with individuals like your co-workers, business associates, or classmates. However, when cultivating those relationships you can chose the level in which you will indulge them into your personal affairs and lifestyle.

Keep in mind that personal information about yourself is just that "personal" and if you divulge your personal information to someone, be sure to think over as to whether you can trust the individual you are sharing it with or if the relationship needs to be further developed. Trust is vital in any relationship and most times it is a factor that can only be cultivated over time.

When evaluating and choosing those whom you will spend a considerable amount of time with; ask yourself if they are of a good influence to you. Do they encourage you to be the best you can be or are they influencing you to engage your vices, bad habits, or weaknesses?

Principle # 9
Evaluate the Company You Keep

If your goal is to reach higher successes than you have ever reached, then you must begin to think in ways that will ignite your passions and align yourself with people who share common interests and who can also inspire you to reach your highest potential. Interestingly enough, people tend to formulate opinions or ideals about one another based on their friends or the company that they keep.

Although we are individuals and unique in our own special way, we still need one another to enhance love in our lives, productivity in our purposes, and support in our daily activities. It is beneficial to align ourselves and befriend those intimately who share common ambitions and aspirations.

> Listed below are some commonly used phrases that acknowledge the power and influence of the "Company You Keep":

"The key is to keep company only with people who uplift you and whose presence calls forth your best."
- Epictetus, Greek Stoic Philosopher

"Be they kings, or poets, or farmers, they're a people of great worth, they keep company with the angels, and bring a bit of heaven here to earth."
- Irish Proverb

"Keep company with good men and you'll increase their number."
- Italian Proverb

Evaluate the Company You Keep

"He who keeps company with wolves will learn to howl."
- Ancient Proverb

"Tell me what company you keep and I'll tell you what you are."
- Miguel de Cervantes Saavedra
(Spanish writer and author of the masterwork 'El Quijote', 1547-1616)

"Turtles will <u>never</u> soar with Eagles... they just don't have the wings to fly."
- Melissa McCloud

IV.

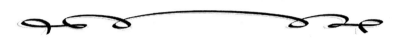

RELEASE THE POWER
WITHIN

"The Power is …

and always has been within you.

Use it!"

- Melissa McCloud

Principle # 10

Love Yourself

Principle # 10
Love Yourself

No one else in the world is identical to you. You have your own unique personality, face, body, and purpose in life. You are one of a kind and an exceptional design. Sometimes it's easy to find things about ourselves that we'd like to change and surely there are some things that we can, but first you must exercise your power to love yourself.

Appreciate your existence and feel comfortable with just being you. Encourage yourself and be your own best friend. Everyday just take a deep breath and say to yourself, "I love me and it is okay to be me." You don't have to try to be something you are not to get people to like you. If they don't like you for who you are then more than likely they will not like you for pretending to be something or someone you are not.

It took a while for me to love myself because for so long I measured my looks and success based on what other people thought of me or by the standard of beauty that I'd see on television and in magazines. I wanted to be slimmer, prettier, more talented, smarter, and more socially popular than I was. I'd focus on what I deemed as my physical flaws and lack of social acceptance rather than focusing on my strengths, talents, and all of the wonderful people and things that I had been rewarded with in life. I had to learn that when I look at myself in the mirror to not focus on what I wish was different about my body but to appreciate all the things that I loved about it!

Many of the fears that I had of what people thought of me dissipated when I realized that God loves me, that I am unique in my own special way, and that I am divinely blessed just the way that I am.

Principle # 10
Love Yourself

You must appreciate who you are and don't ever think of trying to be like someone else.   Be who you are at all times and think of yourself as having qualities and talents whom others can look up to.

 You are extraordinary just the way you are, so congratulate yourself when you have accomplished a goal, celebrate your victories, and remind yourself daily that you are a winner!

Always speak positive words of encouragement that will empower you to continue moving forward in your daily goals. Also, by speaking your positive affirmations daily, you will additionally build your confidence, and when faced with adversity, you will be equipped to act in accordance with your declarations.

Keep in mind that you are loved by God and if you make a mistake or if you do something that you are not proud of, it's okay. Just breathe, forgive yourself, and make an effort to continue to move forward. A key component to loving yourself is forgiving your own mistakes or flaws. Remember that no one is perfect, we all make mistakes but what moves us forward is if we don't permit our mistakes and mishaps to keep us in a constant state of self pity, remorse, and regret. Even God consistently forgives all who ask Him for forgiveness and He never holds our mistakes against us.

Consistently remind yourself that you are priceless and beautiful inside and out, one of a kind, and totally you. Always love yourself and extend loving and encouraging words to those around you.

Love Yourself

Keep in mind that the more you love yourself, the greater you increase your capacity to love others.

No matter your challenges, circumstances, situations, or what others may think or see, you should be a walking example of love-- first by loving yourself and secondly by loving others. The power that lies within giving love and loving yourself, undoubtedly yields an unparalleled force that will help propel you towards being the bold, confident, and fearless person that you were magnificently created to be.

"Love must first dwell within you."
- *Melissa McCloud*

Principle # 11

Forgive Yourself

Forgive Yourself

There were times when I'd find myself being disappointed at what I'd consider my failures, mistakes, or perceived shortcomings. I'd meditate a lot on what I didn't like about myself or what I didn't want to see happen in certain situations in my life. Instead of meditating and dwelling about what I did like about myself or about all of the wonderful things that were happening in my life, I'd choose to badger myself with negative thoughts and words of discouragement that re-emphasized my mistakes. In addition, instead of using my spirit and strength to rise above my adversity and to think of all the progress that I was making in my life, I'd choose to sulk in my frustrations and entertain my doubts and fears.

One day, however, I had an awakening and realized that I must live my life daily in appreciation for all things that God has blessed me with! I began to wholeheartedly realize that the good things in my life heavily outweighed my challenges and fickle circumstances. So, I finally chose to stop thinking about and focusing on past mistakes and regrets.

You see, the truth is, no one is perfect and many people may have something that they may be challenged with overcoming or working to change in their life such as: alcohol abuse, smoking, drugs, low self-esteem, insecurity, fear, gluttony, selfishness, un-forgiveness, conceit, sexual immorality, anger, etc. However, you should not be hard on yourself or put yourself down if you have not yet conquered your vice as soon as you'd like to. Some habits take a lot of time and effort to master and overcome. So, don't be hard on yourself during the process.

Principle # 11
Forgive Yourself

If you experience setbacks in trying to accomplish your goals or digress in your efforts by indulging in the temptations of your vice, then learn from your experiences and disappointments and use them to fuel your continued desires and efforts to thwart your subjugations.

Every day a lesson is learned, a victory is won, a mountain is climbed, and a life is saved. To embrace life without fear, worry, and frustration, you must realize that no matter what happens or how things happen, some things are inevitable and not in your power to control. One of my favorite adages is, "It's not so much what happens to you, but how you react to what happens." You have control and power over your own choices and actions. You have the power to choose how you will respond to your life experiences.

If you made a decision that you regret, please know that every day is a new day and that from this day on you can make new decisions based on your learning experiences and from the tribulations that you have overcome.

The Serenity Prayer:

God grant me the serenity to accept the things that I cannot change. The courage to change the things that I can and the wisdom to know the difference. Amen.

Life is truly a journey and on a journey you may see and experience rain or sunshine, hills or plains, successes or failures, joys and pain, promotions or demotions, and so much more. However, one thing for sure is that within you is the power to learn from and master them all.

Forgive Yourself

You have a choice to live daily knowing that what sometimes may appear as failures, disappointments, and setbacks, were only setups to bring you closer to your ambitions, mission, and purpose in life. When you learn to forgive yourself by not consistently reminding yourself of your perceived failures and shortcomings, you increase your desire to continuously strive to overcome anything that has you bound. The single act of forgiveness or forgiving yourself empowers and releases your inner spirit man to freely grow and move forward with unbound profound power.

Nothing stays the same, things are consistently changing and what you do today will increase your life experiences, magnify your decisions, and fashion your lifestyle for tomorrow. It is never too late to start anew, to set a new goal, and to work towards obtaining the life that you desire. You can choose to forgive yourself today, move forward from past regrets, fears, and pain and onward to live your life with the "spirit of a champion," engaging the wisdom, courage, power, and love that can be found within you to forgive!

Principle # 12

You Deserve the Best

You Deserve the Best

When I was in grade school, high school, and even in college, I experienced verbal abuse from my peers and from some outside of my peer group. Initially, I believed that it really didn't matter what my classmates and peers would say as long as I was not physically harmed or "abused." However, I later realized that negative words which are permeated in verbal abuse would later have more of an impact on my self-esteem, health, thoughts, and long term actions and beliefs than I would expect.

I had never imagined that the power of words could have such an impact on my life. So eventually I learned how to disengage people who did not have my best interest at heart and I learned how to disassociate myself from negative people who were insistent on discouraging me.

Verbal abuse - *Words that attack or injure an individual. Words that cause one to believe an untrue statement, or words that speaks falsely of an individual. (Defined by: Dr. Jay Grady, Ph.D., Stop Verbal Abuse)*

I believe that no one should be subjected to verbal or physical abuse.

Physical abuse - *Abuse involving contact intended to cause feelings of intimidation, pain, injury, or other physical suffering or harm. (As defined in: Wikipedia.org)*

I have found that if someone is verbally or physically abusing you, then they should not be given the privilege of your time,

Principle # 12

You Deserve the Best

friendship, relationship, or any opportunity to continue to be abusive towards you! You deserve the best and you must treat your body and mind with love, tenderness, and kindness consistently re-affirming the greatness that lies within you and releasing the power of confidence and boldness to accept your right to peace and happiness.

"You deserve the best in your relationships."

"You deserve the best in life."

Never accept or believe negative things that people or verbal/physical abusers might say such as: "You'll never amount to anything," " No one will ever love you as much as I do," "You can never escape," "Nobody loves you," "You're ugly and no one will want you," " You are a loser," or "There is no hope for you."

Now I can go on and on with words and phrases verbal and physical abusers might say, but I want you to know that if they have said anything that was just quoted above, then they are telling you lies.

You are not a loser and you are beautiful inside and out. There is hope for you and there are people out there who will love you for you. You can escape physical and verbal abuse, and you can do whatever you set your mind to do because you have the power within you to choose to be happy!

Every last one of us has a choice to embrace and empower ourselves to strive for a fulfilling life with people in it that will celebrate our greatness and uniqueness and who will

You Deserve the Best

encourage us to live a life with love and peace. The world is filled with billions of people and there are people in every state and in every country that can positively increase rewarding relationships in your life!

Never forget to embrace your inner power and willfully reject negative thoughts, words, or actions that align themselves contrary to the empowered man or woman that you have the fortitude and capacity to be!

Remember that you deserve to be happy. You deserve to be celebrated, and you deserve to be free from all forms of abuse. No one has the right to harm you in any way rather it be verbal or physical. Your life has significance and you deserve happiness! Always remind yourself that you are beautifully and wonderfully created. You are a person of destiny and purpose and you deserve the very best that life has to offer!

V.

YOU CAN CHANGE
YOUR LIFE

*"The time to act is now...
what are you waiting for?"*

-Melissa McCloud

Principle # 13

Activate the
Power of Faith

Principle # 13
Activate the Power of Faith

One day I was sitting at the kitchen talking with my father about something that was discomforting to me. I was concerned about a problem that I had absolutely no control over. At that moment, my Dad looked me square in the eyes, quoted a Bible scripture *(found in Proverbs 3:5-6, NIV)* and said, *"Melissa, trust in the Lord with all your heart and lean not to your own understanding. In all your ways acknowledge Him and He shall direct your path."* Now I'd read the scripture before and had heard many people quote it before but for some reason at the moment he said it, something inside of me sparked and from that moment on I've have lived my life accordingly. I have learned to trust in God at all times.

You see, it takes a tremendous amount of courage to have faith that something will change especially when what is visually seen before you appears to be impossible to change. However, the power of faith is ignited when you can trust that the Creator of all things is powerful and can change your life in a moment's time.

Faith - trust in God and in His promises as made through Christ and the Scriptures; Confident belief in the truth, value, or trustworthiness of a person, idea, or thing.

Through my prayers and reading the Bible, I began to understand how it takes faith to please Him, and I knew God heard my prayers, but where I struggled in my faith, was trusting that He would answer my prayers, and that what He promised me would come to pass.

Principle # 13
Activate the Power of Faith

Essentially, I had to grow in the area of knowing God by having a closer relationship with Him, trusting him, knowing that he is in control of my life, and believing that He would withhold no good thing from me. I frequently pray the Lord's Prayer *(found in Matthew 6: 9 -12, NKJV)* to re-confirm and establish in my heart God's omnipotent power and presence in my life.

The scripture reads, "*Our Father which art in heaven, Hallowed be thy name. Thy kingdom come. Thy will be done in earth, as it is in Heaven. Give us this day our daily bread. And forgive us our debts, as we forgive our debtors. And lead us not into temptation, but deliver us from evil: For thine is the kingdom, and the power, and the glory, forever. Amen.*"

I want you to know that if God has promised you something or has spoken to your heart, believe Him. God is not a God that would lie. He is the same yesterday, today, and tomorrow. If He said it, He will do it. Although, bear in mind that it may take some time before his promises manifest. Sometimes our faith and trust in God are tested for a while to see if we will continue to be obedient and faithful to Him during the most difficult times. I believe that is why you see the words "wait and trust" throughout much of the Bible.

Here is a scripture found in *Isaiah 40:31 (NKJV)* that speaks about waiting on the Lord:

Principle # 13
Activate the Power of Faith

"But they that wait upon the LORD shall renew their strength;
they shall mount up with wings as eagles; they shall run, and not
be weary; and they shall walk, and not faint."

I live my life daily trusting God with faith; that He will withhold
no good thing from me, is guiding me, and is with me at all
times.

> *"No good thing will He withhold from them that walk*
> *uprightly."*
> *Psalms 84:11 (NKJV)*

I, as I am sure many others, have had challenges staying in
faith and moving forward with my goals even when the odds
appeared unfavorably against me.

I have learned that it is more advantageous to let go of all
your worries and stress and let God handle the rest. Trust
Him by activating the power of your faith. He already knows
the wonderful things that He has planned for you and He will
show you the way if you just believe.

> *"But without faith it is impossible to please Him: for he that*
> *cometh to God must believe that He is, and that He is a*
> *rewarder of them that diligently seek Him."*
> *Hebrews 11:6 (NKJV)*

Principle # 14

The Power in

Your Prayer

The Power in Your Prayer

I want you to know that when you pray and ask God for guidance He hears you. He knows your heart, your desires, your ambitions, and all of what you are capable of achieving. He knows that at any moment if you would just trust Him with all of your heart and believe that He can do the impossible, then He can change your life in an instant.

Suppose you have been praying for a new job, home, spouse, or a financial blessing. Did you know that God can open up a door of opportunity or send someone to help you when you least expect it? Perhaps, He is waiting for you to trust His guidance; or maybe He has already spoken to your heart and you have not yet completed his instructions.

One thing that I know for sure is that God loves each and every one of us. No matter what we may have done that might have been displeasing to Him, He still cares about us. He is a God of love and forgiveness and primarily what He asks of us is to trust and believe in Him, to be obedient to His Word, and to obey the instructions that He speaks to our hearts. When you surrender your fears, frustrations, worries, and doubts to Him you will find that you will have peace and comfort even when things seem distressing or burdensome. Once you give it all to Him, He will work out the rest.

I can't tell you how many times I have wondered how was I going to make it out of a difficult situation, or how my bills were going to be paid when I had no job, or what was my purpose in life, and when were my wearisome circumstances going to change for the better.

The Power in Your Prayer

However, because I would pray and read the Bible and just ask God to guide me daily, He would comfort my heart and give me peace of mind in the mist of my adversity.

I learned to stop allowing myself to fear based on my impending circumstances. When I stopped worrying and stressing over situations that were not positioned for me to change, my faith was increased, and my life was invigorated.

Because I sought God's guidance I would be assured by Him that He had a divine plan for my life and everything that was happening in my life, no matter if I understood it or not, was guided by His love.

Now I have to admit, there were times when I was challenged with meditating on uncertainties because I didn't understand why things were happening the way they were. But when I wholeheartedly surrendered my will to God's will, I knew that with Him as my guide I couldn't go wrong.

God is sovereign. He knows all and sees all so I had faith that He would omnipotently and divinely direct my path. That is one of the reasons I wrote this book. One day in my prayers I asked God what He wanted me to accomplish next and He put it in my heart to write this book just for you!

Always keep in mind that God hears your prayers even when you think He's not listening, He is! And, even if it takes Him a little while to answer your prayers, while you are waiting, know that He loves you and will never leave you if you would let Him guide you.

The Power in Your Prayer

Perhaps, before He grants you a colossal blessing, He is testing you to see if you will continue to be obedient to His word while in the mist of distress.

Without a doubt, God is forever faithful to His word and true to His unwavering love for all of us. Therefore, you must never stop believing and never stop trusting what God can do in your life. There is power in your prayers and prayers coupled with faith can produce a multitude of blessings!

Principle # 15

Rise Up and

Shine

Principle # 15
Rise Up and Shine

Every day is a new day. Embrace it and choose to be thankful and optimistic. You were born and created to fulfill your destiny and purpose. You can do whatever you set your mind to do. There is no limit to what you can achieve and if you pray and have faith in God, He will definitely see you through.

There is something fantastic about setting goals and objectives, writing them down on paper, and then executing each one of them until you've reached your goal. How exhilarating it feels to finish a project, win a competition, or accomplish personal goals! Now we can all say what we are going to do or what we want to do but there is something about taking your thoughts and goals and putting them into action. So let's get the ball rolling and eliminate procrastination, put your best foot forward, step out on faith with action, conquer your fears, set some goals, and set a timeline to execute each one of them.

Although I've experienced tribulations, circumstances, and challenges in my life, because of my trust and faith in God I have found peace in an unpredictable world. I know that God loves me, is with me, guiding me, and ordering my steps daily. I have learned to trust in God's love and to be grateful no matter what my situations and circumstances are. One thing I know for sure is that nothing stays the same and that everything eventually changes.

You have the power within you to do the unimaginable and reach greater heights than most people wouldn't think possible. You are beautiful inside and out, always believe in yourself, and let no one tell you differently!

Principle # 15
Rise Up and Shine

When you accomplish your objectives it increases your confidence, you become more powerful within, and more than likely you will challenge yourself to achieve greater goals. The more you achieve your goals the more you become self-empowered and enabled to change your state of affairs. Don't let negative thoughts or negative people discourage you from accomplishing what is in your heart.

The time is now! Seize the day. Embrace your life and live it with boldness and confidence knowing that you can accomplish whatever you set your mind to do.

Be determined to live without fear! The power is in you so unleash it and let the world know that you are boldly, confidently, and fearlessly living your life with unwavering faith and great expectancy. Continue to be undoubtedly secure within yourself to love yourself and others genuinely by which leaving an imprint and legacy that can never be erased!

Men and women of destiny and purpose don't be afraid to go for it! Take steps daily toward being bold, confident, and fearlessly you. It is in taking that first step that you will begin to ignite your power within. There is a "you" that has yet to be revealed and is just waiting to burst out and show the world what you are truly made of.

You are beautiful and talented just the way you are and everything that you need to have to be successful and prosperous is already on the inside of you.

Principle # 15
Rise Up and Shine

Act boldly, confidently, and aggressively when in the midst of challenges because you have wholeheartedly resolved that you have the power within you to conquer your fears and succeed at your goals. Let nothing or no one hinder you from following your heart and achieving your dreams-- not fear, doubt, financial setbacks, disappointment, unwanted-circumstances, family, friends, and not even you.

Be prepared to move fearlessly ahead! Be your own coach. Be your greatest motivator and live the best life that you were created to live.

Never doubt yourself and never fear your potential for within you is love and power to achieve greater heights and accomplishments than you could ever imagine.

Give your life the best reward with affirmation and certainty knowing that you have the power and authority to forever live and proclaim "I am bold, I am confident, and I am fearlessly me!"

Now go forth, show the world what you are made of, and be... **Determined to Live without fear!**

VI.

FABULOUS TIPS

&

REMINDERS

"Release your fears, embrace your power, and determine **today** in your mind and in your heart that you are going to complete your goals, dreams, and objectives until the very end!"

- Melissa McCloud

Principle # 16

"Be the Best"

Fabulously You

Tips

"Be the Best": Fabulously You Tips

Be Fabulously the Best!

✦ When you look good, you feel good.

✦ Dress for success every day and put a little strut or swagger into your walk.

✦ Stand up straight with your shoulders squared back and chin up everywhere you go. *(The more you do this the more it will feel natural to you).*

✦ Make sure your hands and feet are always manicured.

✦ Exercise at least three times a week.

✦ Drink eight cups of water daily and prepare healthy foods low in sugar and salt.

✦ Get a minimum of six to seven hours of sleep daily.

✦ Think and say to yourself ten times a day: "I love myself and I have the power within me to get what I want."

✦ Listen to inspirational tapes.

✦ Mediate on your affirmations and positive thoughts daily.

"Be the Best": Fabulously You Tips

✥ Set a daily plan and check off each task as you accomplish your goals.

✥ Make a list of your talents and cultivate them daily.

✥ Be on time to work, school, and to all of your appointments and engagements.

✥ Always greet people with a smile-- you'd be amazed at how much your smile can brighten someone's day.

✥ Make eye contact when engaging in conversation with others.

✥ Say to yourself daily, "I am Bold, Confident, and Fearlessly me!"

✥ Never put yourself down...Everyone is different and has a valuable contribution to make to a diverse society...you are important for the person you are.

✥ Act confident, even if you don't truly feel it. After a while, it will come naturally, and you will feel confident in yourself!

✥ Change up your look. ..Whether you're male or female, getting a new outfit and hairstyle can make you feel fresh, vivacious, cool, and confident.

"Be the Best": Fabulously You Tips

⊕ Speak your personal affirmations daily.

⊕ Work daily to strengthen your talents and skills.

⊕ *Think Big!* There is nothing too great or too small that can't be done!

⊕ Know that you are a valuable person with much to offer to the world around you.

⊕ Keep yourself grounded and surrounded with positive people and things.

⊕ Say this affirmation to yourself every day: "I am beautifully and wonderfully made."

Principle # 17

Melissa's Quotes to Remember

Melissa's Quotes to Remember

"Believe in yourself...you can change your life!"

"Everything that you need to be successful and to follow your dreams is already on the inside of you."

"Love yourself, think positive, and know without a shadow of doubt that nothing is impossible to them that believe."

"Know without a shadow of doubt that you deserve the best that life has to offer."

"Turtles will never soar with Eagles... they just don't have the wings to fly."

"Determine the foods, exercises, and activities that make you feel healthy and physically empowered and make your choices accordingly."

"Love must first dwell within you."

"You deserve to be celebrated!"

"Encourage yourself and be your own best friend."

"Disassociate yourself from verbal and physical abusers."

"Remind yourself daily that you are loved by God."

Melissa's Quotes to Remember

"You have the power to listen to your body and to prove to yourself that you have the determination, courage, and tenacity to see your goals through."

"There is great purpose in your life, so you must trust your instincts, align with your higher spiritually guided self, and know that you were intently created and formed to live a life filled with purpose and that "purpose" is found in God."

"Encourage yourself and be your own best friend."

"Disassociate yourself from verbal and physical abusers."

"Remind yourself daily that you are loved by God."

"You must never stop believing and never stop trusting what God can do in your life. There is power in your prayers and prayers coupled with faith can bring about change with a multitude of blessings!"

"You deserve the best in life."

"Release your fears, embrace your power, and determine today in your mind and in your heart that you are going to complete your goals, dreams, & objectives until the very end."

"Yes you can and yes you will succeed."

"Unwavering faith brings about an expedient change."

Principle # 17

Melissa's Quotes to Remember

"The time is now! Seize the day. Embrace your life and live it your way."

"It is the little steps daily that brings about the greatest changes infinitely!"

"It is necessary that you maximize your time so that it is used productively because; what you do today determines the outcomes of your tomorrow and how you make daily use of your time is vital to your success!"

"A short moment of indulgence can cause a longer time of restoration."

"Remember, don't give up, don't give in, and don't you dare quit because you just may be getting closer to the promotion and reward that living a fearless life can bring."

"The choice is always yours…choose wisely."

"Remember success begins with you!"

Principle # 18

"Move Forward" The World is waiting for you

"Move Forward": The World is waiting for you

Congratulations! If you are reading this page and have read this entire book, then you are now ready to boldly, confidently, and fearlessly live your life! You know that you have the power to create in your life daily what you'd like to see accomplished or changed, and that nothing is impossible to them that believe and go for it!

Everything that you need to be successful is already on the inside of you! Remember to starve your fears, demolish your doubts, put God first in your life, and prove to yourself and to the world around you that you can accomplish anything that you set your mind to do!

You are mentally and physically content because you are fabulously you, you love yourself, and you listen to your body. Also, you know how to release your power from within because you believe in yourself enough to utilize your talents to boldly show the world what you are made of.

Additionally, you've mastered conquering your fears because you realize that you have the power to choose to be the best "you" that you can be and you will never quit! You know that in all things God loves you and through faith and prayer you can change your life. You are now ready to change your life, live your dreams, listen to your heart, and seize divine opportunities as they come your way.

If you have read this book then I can honestly say that you have been pre-destined to make a change and difference in your life and in the lives of others.

Principle # 18

"Move Forward": The World is waiting for you

This book was written especially for you. And, whether if you agree or disagree with all of the content herein, please know that from the depths of my heart, I believe that you can live a life filled with love, joy, peace, and happiness.

Read this book often, let it speak to your heart, and read and say aloud your affirmations daily. By boldly, confidently, and fearlessly living your life, you will experience a freedom and comfort that supersedes the limitations of negative thinking, self-doubt, and fear.

And, because you are secure in your ability and power to conquer all fear; no one can take the confidence you've nurtured within. Remember, don't get discouraged, don't doubt, don't quit, and don't you fear. It is time to step into your new season of life because you are now **determined to live without fear!**

"It is your time to shine...Illuminate!"
-Melissa McCloud

MelissaMcCloud.com